How it all began

We need no reminder about the pace of change in society. What once felt so settled has disappeared with no reference to our preferences. The disconnect between the elite and the rest has never seemed so distant. And so it was fifty years ago. The centre of Sandgate was thriving with both sides of the High Street full of busy shoppers. It was a time when businesses such as butchers, banks, wet fishmongers, tobacconists, confectionery shops and hardware outlets all had their loyal customers. Crossing the road was no problem and it was certainly a social occasion to pass time with acquaintances. By the early 60s there came a subtle change. It was the start of progress as towns were seduced by the promise of a fresh clean future with sparkling shopping centres and speedy travel on three lane motorways. We could discover another town - but the centre looked remarkably similar to the jaded one we left half an hour ago. Novelty replaced stability.

VILLAGERS FIGHT TO SAVE INN

By 1962 the south coast holiday trade was also in a state of change. Two Folkestone hotels, the Majestic and the Queen's, closed during that year. The Royal Kent Hotel in Sandgate was also struggling. Proprietor Christopher Fyson declared that Folkestone was finished as a holiday resort. "We have been full this year on only two weeks. We can't run a business on that basis." Planning permission for demolition had been granted in May 1961, but publicity surrounding the closure and loss of such a huge presence on the High Street polarised opinion. A concerned group of individuals in the village galvanised around antiques dealer Ruby Greenwall who wanted a preservation order placed on the 18th century hotel.

Another less noticed event had slipped through in January 1962. An application was made to demolish the 16th century Sandgate Castle and replace it with 3 blocks of

SANDGATE CASTLE APPLICATION

Block of flats on site proposed

flats. Although the proposal was rejected, it was a signal that the shape and atmosphere of the village was under serious threat. The formation of the Sandgate Preservation Society was a sign that the village was finally fighting back.

Fifty years on, the Society retains its role as guardian of Sandgate's well being. This book chronicles the battles, won and lost, and the continuing vigilance needed to preserve the best of the old while encouraging sympathetic and responsible redevelopment.

From the Patron of the Sandgate Society

Having worked in Sandgate for much of my life, I think I can claim a real connection with the place. Its setting, right by the sea, is at the same time dramatic and picturesque, and is probably what attracts most people to live and work here. It can be as exhilarating a place during a winter storm as it is idyllic on long summer days. There is a strong sense of history here, and although the years have brought about many changes, it is still recognisably the same village depicted in postcards from the nineteenth century. There are many notable and historic buildings, and others from the more recent past that are equally distinctive; all of them contribute to a surprisingly rich variety of architecture. Above all, though, it is a place with a strong sense of community, that feels comfortable and welcoming, and that embraces change and maint

Best v  laan CBE DL

This publication is dedicated to the memory of Ruby Greenwall and her founding team, as well as the Presidents, Chairmen and committee members who have served the Sandgate Society and the village community for the past 50 years.

Acknowledgements. Help with research and production was generously offered by the Society's Chairman, Roger Joyce, the Committee, the Archive team, Folkestone Heritage Room, the Folkestone Estate, Folkestone Herald, Andrea Rubin, Bobbie Allen, Graham Turnill, J & J Print, Liz Joyce, Peter Heselden, Ray Holland, Rosie Unsworth, Past Presidents - Linda René-Martin and Reginald Turnill and all editors of the Society Newsletter.

Photographic acknowledgements - Dolphin pictures courtesy of Terry Whittaker (terrywhittaker.com), Ray Holland for Little Theatre images, FPDsavills and to Chris Phillips for general shots from his vast collection of Sandgate ephemera.

Most of the photographs have been donated to the archive over the decades and sadly many contain no specific year or copyright holdings. We apologise in advance if any copyright has been infringed.

Editor Bob Preedy

This publication has been made possible by generous grants from the Roger De Haan Charitable Trust, Reginald & Margaret Turnill, Linda René-Martin, Ann Nevill and Euan Williamson.

Introduction from our Chairman

I am proud to be serving as Chairman at this important time in the Society's history. Coming to work in Hythe in 1972, and commuting from Rochester before committing to a permanent move to this area, I moved to Sandgate in 1974, and gravitated to the wonderful Antique shops that were there at the time. Ruby Greenwall's was of course one of the most important, and her magnetic personality guaranteed that revisits would be frequent...

Ruby soon discovered that I was an Architect, interested in the historic environment and suggested I join her Committee, which must have been in its twelfth year at the time.

I remember some of the amazing characters that were forming the bedrock of a strong Amenity Society 'with a mission'. The loss of the Kent Hotel was fresh in their minds, and the newly built flats on the site had become part of the 'new Sandgate'. The Sandgate Study was an innovative document, produced around that time, and two Conservation Areas had been designated, largely through the efforts of Linda René-Martin. These were pioneering days in the history of the Conservation movement. I recall that Anthony Swaine was 'honorary Architect' to the Society – almost certainly someone whom Ruby had persuaded to add his weight and experience to the early work of the Society. Tony had been responsible for 'saving' Faversham's centre, and establishing one of the country's first Conservation Areas there. He later became the Conservation Officer for Margate, writing the definitive history and study of the Old Town in the 1970s. So we had a good mentor in the beginning....

Of passing interest is my introduction to Tony by Ruby, and the subsequent years I spent as an Associate of his Canterbury-based practice, before setting up on my own in 1977.

Almost 40 years of practically continuous service on the Committee has proved interesting – I have seen Sandgate transformed from an Antiques mecca, to what is fast becoming a gastronomic centre.

I naturally took on the planning role within the committee, and have seen some quite interesting cases, from a minor debate about replacement windows, to the fight to save 'Enbrook', a Listed building by S.S. Teulon, with later modifications and extensions by Edwin Cooper, one time president of the RIBA. I was around when the Village sign was commissioned (and paid for) by the Society, and helped set up the 'Festival Committee' in the Queen's Jubilee year, bringing in designers with whom I was working, to produce quality products....

I recall the threat to the Branch Library, when KCC decided to build the present one, and to dispose of the Old Fire Station. What may have become a steak restaurant for the adjacent Whitbread pub, was saved by a group of residents who formed the Sandgate Heritage Trust Ltd. The Trust was then able to secure the services of the Youth Opportunities Scheme and, advised by our excellent antiques dealers, we all supervised the restoration of the unique Reading Room, installing reproduction lamps where the old gas lamp conduits were uncovered behind removable pilasters.

Before the creation of the Parish Council in 2004, the Sandgate Society did most things, persuading and cajoling the Local Authority as necessary – and not always without heated discussion....it was somewhat of a relief to be part of the discussion surrounding the Parish Council, which we welcomed, as the tasks undertaken by the local community could now be shared out. Now I think we have an excellent working relationship with the Parish Council.

With no 'official' mechanism in place to create quasi-establishments , early committees (such as the Silver Jubilee Week of celebrations), became the 'Sea Festival Committee', and Twinning, a splendid idea from Ann Nevill and some of us on the Committee, became independent with the blessing of the Local Authority.

There has always been a healthy social side of Committee work, which spills out into the wider membership, and to the community. The Saturday coffee mornings, the annual garden party, (started by Reg and Margaret Turnill) and the Christmas Party, that began as a 'mince pie and mulled wine' evening hosted in the Chichester Hall (its saviour, Geoffrey Edmunds), have become an established part of village life, and enjoy a legendary reputation.

I believe the Society has a bright future, and will fulfil an ever greater role, with the onset of 'Localism', and the 'Big Society', when the pressure to develop our coastline will never go away. We need to protect our heritage, guard our Conservation Areas, and continue to take a healthy interest in matters relating to the changing Local Plans.....

This souvenir publication attempts to capture a flavour of the history that has shaped our village, some of the personalities that have made the Society, and to create a 'snapshot' of the past 50 years of its life. I believe the centenary publication will come to make a fascinating companion volume.

Roger A Joyce, RIBA 2012

"Sandgate? Pull it down and start afresh! That's what I call future planning." - December 1963

"A landmark in Sandgate is going. Demolition of the Royal Kent Hotel is well in hand. The property is in an area scheduled for redevelopment."

It revealed to the villagers that they had a seafront. I do not think they realised it before. Ugly buildings have always hidden the sea. This problem is partly solved by the present demolitions. If we wait a little longer, no doubt the rest will fall by decay." An anonymous letter writer to the Herald, signing himself as S.H.L. opined that "the village consisted of a heterogeneous collection of low grade architecture, much of which is in a very sorry state of repair. To try to preserve this "character" is utter nonsense and a wicked waste of money."

Antique dealer Frank Norden captured the growing unease in the village, "We must advance bravely with the times for these are the years of progress – with space travel, Bingo, the Twist and that highly rewarding but most exclusive sport called speculative building - played to the advantage of some and the disillusionment of many. It is a fast game so keep your eye on the ball."

So said Councillor J. C. Hughes during the Folkestone Council debate after the publication of Noel Tweddle's report into the redevelopment of Sandgate. A year after formation the Sandgate Society was to feel the full Folkestone fury. The sympathetic 13 page report referred to the widening to 74 feet of the A259, which he said could destroy the village unless an alternative route was found. He also foresaw that car parking would be an increasing headache for the village. He concluded his report by saying that Sandgate could never become more than a ribbon of development about a mile long and 100 yards wide, sandwiched between the steeply enclosing hills and the sea. But he added "No town stands still. It either grows or decays. In my perambulation of Sandgate, there are signs of both, with decay predominating. It gave me the impression of relying too much on its history and not welcoming the future."

In the December 1963 Folkestone council debate, Ald. A. Sainsbury advised that "Sandgate should stop thinking of itself as a separate entity but as one of the impressive approaches to Folkestone, the premier seaside resort on the South Coast."

Councillor J.H. Sainsbury continued the onslaught, "The knocking down of the Royal Kent Hotel was one of the greatest services ever performed for Sandgate.

"Nearly the end of the former Bevan Military Hospital, and, later, nursing home, Sandgate. Our picture was taken from the sea side. In the background, through the aperture, is the main road."

1963 *At the first AGM the Sandgate Heritage Trust is renamed the Sandgate Society. Along Sandgate High Street you could find 57 thriving businesses. The Ministry of Transport plans a new route through the village and the council is given a building line for road widening. The Military Tavern closes after last orders on Monday 10th June. Two landmarks are demolished - The Royal Kent Hotel in January and the Bevan Nursing Home by October.*

The Military Tavern: Replaced by the Green and a car park.

Colonel Murphy enjoys a fanfare with his pupils (from left to right) brothers Abdul Moteb bin Abdul bin Saud, Abdul Tajeed bin Saud, Abdul Mohsin bin Saud and Fawaz bin Saud - Saudi Princes.

1964 *Advertisers want to erect hoardings on the Military Tavern site, but the Society suggests landscaping and a few seats. 15 new shops are included in the Sandgate redevelopment plans. In May Colonel Desmond Henry Murphy acquires Encombe for use as a language school. Sandgate's Reservoir in Cliff Road, Seabrook is turned off in February. The Congregational Church closes in June after its Sunday attendance diminishes to just eight.*

1965 *A campaign starts to open the walkway to the public from Radnor Cliff to Folkestone but this is owned by the Radnor Estate and the council has no control over the access. A history exhibition about Sandgate, opened by actor David Tomlinson, for a week in August attracts 1000 visitors to the Chichester Hall. Part of the Castle is offered to the village for use as a museum.*

Encombe: Recollections from Linda René-Martin

This estate is best described as an enchanted terrain beset by unlovely events. The 1893 landslide wrecked many Sandgate properties over a very wide area, and then came the greedy and damaging developments in the 1960s, a mysterious fire in 1978 and today, a large scale development in abeyance.

The very name, Encombe, stirs family memories. In 1932, no sooner had my somewhat eccentric grandfather bought a leasehold Coastguard Cottage at auction, than he had ambitions to own a country estate and set his sights on Encombe.

Four years earlier Ralph Philipson, coal magnate and patron of the arts, had died. For his gifted widow Maya the gilded life and circle at Encombe had faded and she wanted to sell. In a hired Rolls Royce my impecunious grandfather rolled up the winding driveway, flanked by two bronze hinds, to the summit of his ambitions and tea with Mrs. Philipson.

Together with his dear Irish terrier, Bob, he would regale us with an update while his cronies at the national Liberal Club thought him a secret millionaire which he certainly wasn't. My mother pleaded with his Haymarket bank not to lend him any money. The manager replied, "Oh I haven't the heart to refuse the dear old gentleman." We dreaded the thought we might inherit Encombe and all his debts.

One day he told us that Mrs. Philipson had at last agreed to accept his offer of £25,000 – the only stipulation was that she should leave the kitchen fully equipped – he thought this was the one thing needed when taking over an empty house – was this a frying pan too far? At that she stalled and the deal fell through. Great was the family relief.

Encombe sparks another memory. In the early 1960s the Sandgate Society raised a howl and rightly so when the noise and danger of speedboats and water skiers close inshore had become a danger and an infernal nuisance to beach lovers and residents alike. We needed bye-laws and the Folkestone Town Clerk was dragging his feet. Ruby Greenwall instigated a mass petition and volunteers were given areas to canvass. Working full time in London, I had come down to the cottage for a quiet weekend. But not a bit of it. My stint covered the Coastguard, the Esplanade and Encombe areas.

With some trepidation I toiled up the Encombe driveway, passed the ornamental well in the forecourt and knocked on the heavy studded doors of the still lovely mansion. Here a Colonel Murphy of the Glubb Pasha brigade wing was running a school for about 100 boys from the Middle East to learn English and enlarge their education. Encombe, as we know, is set in a natural amphitheatre, and all the more is a noise trap. Not only did the Colonel sign with alacrity, he also asked all his boys to sign as well. Four of them were Saudi Arabian princes I now know. Later in the 1960s the Encombe area gave rise to great concern. Earth movement had been reactivated when a consortium of Folkestone developers and builders had managed to obtain Council permission to redevelop the estate, wreck the landscape and ornamental water gardens and even get the dead end driveway adopted as a public road.

Just before Christmas neighbours on the Coastguard phoned me in London to say our walls were cracking up and I should return to Sandgate at once. A determined newcomer, Alex Todd, and myself, with the Society's backing, eventually forced the Folkestone Council to face up to the serious situation that placed residential and public property at risk.

A public meeting was eventually organised with Mayor Bancroft in the chair. Councillors, technical staff and a senior partner from Halcrows, John Muir Wood, gathered to put our fears to rest. Of course the hillside was running with springs, as I showed MP Albert Costain on a personal safari, because the water gardens had been wrecked. The Sandgate Laundry in the Wilberforce area, boasting "we wash your linen in pure spring water" drew over 100,000 gallons of water each week, but had recently burnt down. Consequently a vast amount of water was permeating the strata and forcing its way to the sea. "Oh", said the Halcrow man, "It's no more that a bathful of water per person a day." That's all right I said, as long as you pull out the plug. Loud laughter temporarily lightened the atmosphere.

Catching the train back to London I noticed there was John Muir Wood on the platform too. He gave up his first class apartment to seat himself in mine. This was an ideal opportunity to pick his brain, but of course he was in the Council's employ and I couldn't presume. One nugget emerged however. When the Abbey National bought Encombe as a holiday home, their chairman called in Halcrows to advise. "I told him," said my fellow passenger, "he would not only need an umbrella (the Abbey logo) but galoshes too." That said it all.

1966 *The Beach Marine Hotel is demolished in March. Summer concern about the noise and danger from speed boats leads to a petition and a change in bye-laws. During this, the H.G.Wells centenary year, four films of his work are shown in September. Two bronze hinds each weighing 1cwt and then worth £140 are stolen from the gateposts of Encombe Estate.*

Encombe House: Destroyed in 1978 by a mysterious fire

Hinds: Metal thieves stole the beautiful bronze models at the Entrance Gate

Revealed: The petrol station's demolition shines light on the Gough Road Methodist Church which is still visible after the new Service Station opens for trade - with Double Green Shield Stamps.

1967 In February a major landslip affects the Encombe and Coastguard Cottages area. A man-made explosion in July rocks the area during a salvage operation to explode a WW2 boat holding explosives. Caffyn's garage site is cleared and used as a car park. The James Morris Dwellings are considered unsafe and may be demolished. A storm path from Encombe to Sandgate village is proposed in case of lower level flooding. Sandgate Motors Garage is demolished in February, and the new Amoco station opens on 30th December.

Devonshire Terrace, Sandgate.   H.B's.Fsn. No.702

(top)
Devonshire
Terrace: Battered
by the weather
and removed by
the wrecking crew.

(below)
Low Spirits:
Another popular
outlet disappears,
the Valentine
Charles Wine Store
conveniently next
to the Ship Inn.

1968 February sees the Victorian Devonshire Terrace reduced to rubble. After years of battering from the elements the terrace was in a dangerous condition. The first pint is pulled at a new Golden Valley pub, the Golden Arrow – named after the crack boat train. Action is taken by Alex Todd to protect the old Encombe Ice Well. The front door of the now demolished Royal Kent Hotel is in the possession of Mrs. Collins of 3 Wellington Terrace. The High Street is flooded during November. The Valentine Charles Wine Store, adjacent to the Ship Inn, is demolished in August. Sixty detectives probe a mystery death at the Dolphin Guest House, 5 High Street. Dog fight sequences for the 1969 film, The Battle of Britain, are shot over Sandgate bay using just nine repainted planes from the Spanish Air Force. Flats replacing the Beach Marine Hotel are nearing completion.

The Royal Kent Hotel coffee room.

Frozen in Time: Two evocative images of the High Street taken from the partly demolished Royal Kent Hotel.

The massive Bevan Nursing Home dominated the Sandgate seafront.

High Street: The Post Office.

Skyscraper: Just imagine...

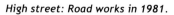

High street: Road works in 1981.

Beach Marine Hotel: Demolished in March 1966.

1969 The Woodford Hotel is regarded as in a dangerous condition. Public toilets open on Granville Parade. Kenneth Higgins the owner of Rayner's Beach Club proposes a futuristic Skyscraper tower, 26-storey and 280ft high, which will span the road and cost £1m. Lister Way between Sandgate Hill and Castle Road is named after Councillor Charles Lister. The site of Sandgate's 110 year old reservoir in Cliff Road, Seabrook is to be sold for development.

Cliff House

Cliff House and Palm Beach – "The choicest locations"

One house lasted 140 years, the other a mere 50. Both were regarded as the most desirable of addresses, with their position described as "isolated from the world and completely secluded." Built on Radnor Estate land in 1829 for Captain Gill, Cuma Place was situated at the eastern end of Lower Sandgate Road, this side of the Toll House. By 1835 it was referred to as Cliff House and was occupied by many distinguished families who enjoyed the solitude and the stunning uninterrupted Channel views. Originally built in an almost square shape jutting into the extensive 5 acre grounds, it was twice remodelled.

Folkestone and Hythe MP Stewart Marjoribanks was here from 1837 to 1842, after which he became the leading promoter of the Folkestone Gas Company. William Pearth then took residence until his death in 1854. General Henry Hankey arrived at Cliff House in 1859 and stayed here with his wife Emily until his death in 1886. His widow resided for a further nine years and died in 1895. The remaining 43 year lease

The Manor House

The Earl's new residence on the Folkestone Leas

was then purchased by Mr. and Mrs D. Lionel Thomson who gave much pleasure to local children by holding summer parties in the magical grounds.

Up on the Leas, in the Manor House, built in 1896, the 6th Lord Radnor was struggling to accommodate his family of eight children. He therefore bought back the Estate's own lease on Cliff House in December 1906 and soon added an extension that ran eastwards along the line of the road. This L shaped house now provided much needed nursery space for his young family. The presence of Lord & Lady Radnor can only have added to the immense status of living on the Radnor Cliff and Riviera enclave.

The family was here for nearly two decades as the children grew up, but in 1926 there was a change to the lease. The Earl's "tenant for life" clause was removed and a henceforth unencumbered freehold was offered for sale.

Cliff House then entered a decade long merry go round of ownership by rich widows. Purchasing the

1970 *There was much discussion in the village about acquiring the toll road from the Radnor Estate, but Lower Sandgate Road is in need of considerable repair. Dr. Courtney Lendon comes to Sandgate and takes over the Lachlan medical practice. Helena Hospital closes in April. Plans by Fredack Investments Ltd to demolish Shorncliffe Lodge and build a four storey block of 16 flats are thwarted.*

freehold which included the house, 5 acres of land, two cottages and stabling garage for £13,000 in 1927 was Mrs Marion Ada Johnstone. Written into her sale contract was the freedom to demolish or alter any structure she so desired on the large estate, which also held extensive land on the north side of Lower Sandgate Road. Up to 1927 the road was known as Clifton Place – then both sides became Radnor Cliff, with odd numbers to the north and even on the south side.

Mrs. Johnstone certainly used her tenure as a very skilful estate developer. Her first move in January 1927 was to demolish the original square shaped western end of the L shaped house. In its place was a continuation of the lateral extension added by Lord Radnor. The conservatory, slightly further west, was incorporated as the southern part of the present day Sea Spray house. On the north side of the road, replacing a former kitchen garden was Well House, built in 1933. To the east of this she added Green Harbour in 1935, and soon moved there, selling Cliff House for £20,000 to widow Mrs. Charrington following the death of husband Henry, near neighbours at 16 Radnor Cliff. A year later in 1938 Mrs. Charrington sold the house to her daughter Mrs Nancy Furlong, wife of Brigadier Dennis Furlong who died in action in September 1940. Before the 1937 sale the Cliff House estate was divided into two, such that the east end of the house marked the boundary. On the remaining far eastern parcel Mrs Johnstone created the delightful Palm Beach, with completion in 1939.

Cliff House and gardens

Joining Mrs. Furlong at Cliff House in April 1941 was her new husband Sir John Greer Dill. Sir John lived until 1944 and Lady Dill remained at Cliff House for a

further four years when Thomas S. Wilding bought it for £20,000. He created a stylish water garden – a part of which still survives. His actor son, Michael was married to Elizabeth Taylor from 1952 to 1956 – and the film superstar is known to have stayed at Cliff House.

By the late 1960s the house was split into apartments and was eventually sold for £50,000 in 1971 to R.A. Muddle, managing director of Peacock's Ford Garage in Folkestone. The house was soon demolished and after long planning delays the present modern blocks of Cliff House apartments were occupied on 999 year leases from 1992.

Palm Beach was purchased in 1947 by Victor Behar who later ran the Beach Marine Hotel on the Riviera. He died in 1965 leaving an estate valued at £198,298. Palm Beach was sold in 1987 and replaced by Marine Point by July 1991.

An era of gracious living had ended.

Sandgate's First 10 Telephone Numbers.

1. Simonds Brewers, High Street
2. Sir Squire Bancroft, Underlea
3. F.G. Davison, Garage, Shorncliffe Camp
4. County Police Station, Seabrook
5. Officers' Mess, 87th Regiment, Moore Barracks.
6. Officers' Mess, King's Royal Rifles, Napier Barracks
7. War Office, Shorncliffe Military Exchange
8. Philip Sassoon, Shorncliffe Lodge
9. G & E Swaffer, Corn Merchants, Horn Street Mill
10. Post Office, 76 High Street. The Public Call box at 72 High Street was No.14

1971 *The council is offered the Methodist Church in Gough Road for use as a library or Day Care Centre. Cliff House, built around 1829, is demolished with plans for replacement by town houses and yachtsmen's homes with boat storage. A second public telephone box is requested for the growing village of Sandgate.*

Radnor, Rothschild & Sassoon

This is a 19th century story of power and money involving a landowner, a Military General and high profile MPs.

Around 1784 a major landslip created an undulating strip of land along the coast from Sandgate to Folkestone. Lord Radnor was then able to create Lower Folkestone Road in 1824 (known as Lower Sandgate Road from 1875) as a means of avoiding the hill out of Folkestone harbour. Both of these were controlled by Toll Booths - the first in the garden of a one-time Radnor house, Endcliffe, Sandgate Hill which in 1838 produced a net toll profit of £561.

In 1839 MP Stewart Marjoribanks took a Radnor lease on a parcel of choice land near to the second Toll Booth on the Undercliff, later known as Radnor Cliff. The lease ran from Michaelmas Day (29th September) 1839 for 99 years. A connected piece of land was also leased by William Pearth for the same period. It is believed that on the site from 1829 was Cuma Place built for, or occupied by, Captain Charles Gill. By 1835 it was known as Cliff House with local MP Stewart Marjoribanks the occupier from 1837.

William Pearth then took residence from 1842 to his death in 1854. Whether Cuma Place was demolished or simply renamed as Cliff House is unclear.

Later in that decade Colonel Henry Aitcheson Hankey stood for election in the constituency but lost to Sir John Ramsden, a major Northern landowner. In 1859 Hankey tried again but he and all other candidates were persuaded to step aside and allow unopposed success for Baron Mayer de Rothschild. The oath "on the true faith of a Christian" had kept Jews out of parliament but, following intense lobbying by Lionel, Mayer's brother, and Benjamin Disraeli, Leader of the Commons, the oath was amended for their inclusion from 1858. Shortly afterwards Colonel Hankey took a long lease on Cliff House.

On Baron Rothschild's death in May 1874, his daughter Hannah, now the richest woman in the country, gifted a lifeboat as a memory of her father. This was housed in the later so called Goose

Beyond the Lifeboat Station on Hospital Hill are the Military Hospitals. The "Goose Cathedral" later became the Life-Boat Cafe before being demolished in 1956 and replaced with a petrol station.

James Morris building: Declared as slums and replaced by housing and the library.

1972 After a protracted campaign the Society wins two large Conservation and six Tree Preservation Areas across the village, in the face of much opposition from Folkestone Borough Council. The Woodford Hotel and the 1876 James Morris Building are both demolished this year. Sandgate's High Street was highly commended by judges of the Illustrated London News competition for the Best Decorated Jubilee Street. The Methodist Church in Gough Road is set to close.

The Benvenue: Under the waves opposite The Sandgate Hotel.

the next two decades. During his time as MP for the area he opened and maintained a free dental clinic in Folkestone as well as building a model working class housing estate of 16 cottages and 8 flats in East Cliff. After his death in 1939 his sister Sybil inherited the estate and in 1946 she sold out to a property company. In 1973 John Aspinall offered £400,000 for the Port Lympne estate. The Sassoon house remains a stunning centrepiece at this popular Wild Animal Park.

Philip Sassoon MP.

Cathedral on the Sandgate/Seabrook border and its final heroic act was to rescue the crew of the Benvenue in the powerful storm of 11th November 1891. The crew included Fred Moore's father, Thomas, who received a medal for bravery. The lifeboat was later stationed at Folkestone but was surplus to requirements. A suggestion to use it as a gondola on the Radnor Park pond was rejected and it was sold by the Corporation in 1894 for £5.

Sir Edward Watkin was the next MP and during his occupancy he clearly saw the potential for extending his railway line from Sandgate to Folkestone. However, ferocious opposition from the landowner and his new residents on Radnor Cliff curtailed this fanciful scheme.

In 1887 Sir Edward Sassoon took a bride who may have been familiar with this area – he had sensibly chosen Aline Caroline de Rothschild, a French cousin of Hannah, daughter of Mayer de Rothschild. Sir Edward was elected as MP for Hythe and Folkestone in 1899 and shortly afterwards the couple made their home in Sandgate's Shorncliffe Lodge, taking a 7 year lease from the Countess of Chichester. Their second child Sybil eventually married, outside the faith, the 5th Marquess of Cholmondeley, the Earl of Rocksavage. Her older brother Philip declined marriage but gained much satisfaction by taking over his father's Parliamentary seat in 1912.

A millionaire at the age of 23 he used his inheritance to create, with architect Sir Herbert Baker, the magnificent Port Lympne, home to much gaiety over

The Rothschild connection lived on in the area. The Hon. Miss E. Rothschild was in residence at Beaulieu on the Riviera from 1966 to 1971. Her chauffeur used to drive the Rolls-Royce over to Ron Tabor's High Street butchers shop to collect the weekly meat order.

1973 Two old Pub signs are found near the derelict Rayner's Beach Club. Both the Old Rose and the Royal Oak signs are now displayed in the old Fire Station. A letter in the Herald expresses concern that antique dealers are taking over the village. A battle looms over the future of the 1866 Church of England Primary School.

1974 In May partial demolition of Shorncliffe Lodge is halted after the Society initiates Grade II "spot listing", after planning permission is sought for conversion to flats. Yellow No parking lines are extended over most of the High Street shopping area. Restoration of the Castle starts and will continue for 14 years.

Over now to our BBC aerospace correspondent, Reg Turnill...

Margaret and I arrived by chance in Sandgate in 1976, and had a splendid salmon salad lunch facing a sunlit sea at the Miles Haven wine bar, later Bar Vasa. The landlady there introduced us to the owner of Somerville Lodge, a recently-listed house opposite the Coastguard Cottages. Almost every room had glorious views across the Channel and within half an hour we knew that was to be our retirement home. It had Kent-peg tiles on the roof, and if you touched them when inside the attic, they slid off in a shower. It had no foundations, and sat on some old ships' timbers placed on the clay floor. And its ancient electrical system was life-threatening.

It took several years, and nine months of bitter feuding with the Shepway District Council, who hated the prospect of us making the 200-year-old house habitable, before we had sorted it all out. But we found a marvellous worker living on the Romney Marsh who was unfazed at the problems of installing foundations beneath a house already standing.

In 38 years since, we have never regretted coming to Sandgate, despite a few ups and downs. In the early years there was a reliable 75-minute train service to London. Having been retired from my staff job on the BBC, I was able to continue my journalistic life as an aerospace freelance reporter commuting between London studios and US space centres like Cape Canaveral and Houston, covering the manned space flights and Concorde. At our house, a north-facing room, away from the distracting views of Cape Gris-Nez and the French coastline, became my office, where I wrote scripts for Newsround, and slowly assembled 14 books.

Finding a doctor proved difficult, but Courtney Lendon, who was to be Sandgate's last local GP, finally took us on his panel - though he hinted it was conditional upon our becoming members of both the English Speaking Union and the Sandgate Society. Courtney practised, together with Dr. Fritz Ewer, from The Crescent, and their prescriptions kept Chaplin's well-run pharmacy going.

Opposite, in what is now Escondido, was Halletts, an invaluable hardware store, whose vast stock was stored in brick vaults running beneath it.

Sandgate certainly needed its civic society. Back streets like The Crescent and Wilberforce Road were pretty seedy. As in our case the houses needed much attention. And there were ruthless developers around, careless of the fact that bulldozing on the hillsides could and did start landslides. We had discovered the hard way that insurance companies were reluctant to provide cover in what had been designated "a slippage area" since the 1890s. We learned about that from an outspoken resident called Alex Todd. He made headlines in the early days of TV news doing an interview beside his house on the Encombe Estate. He kept a caravan stocked with food and water, he explained, against the inevitable day when Sandgate would slide into the sea – unless something was done. For some years after that few wanted to buy a Sandgate house and an unpopular Todd moved to Hythe.

But a few years later he returned, and his legacies include a traditional and now very rare ice house which he excavated beside the storm path leading from the Wilberforce car park to Encombe. They were used to store dry ice before plentiful electricity enabled anyone with a fridge to make their own ice. Despite its rarity and tourist value, he could get no one interested; so to preserve it for a future more enlightened generation he carefully re-filled it with garden rubbish. It's still there, awaiting the day when it is rediscovered.

And of course, millions have since been spent making Sandgate's esplanade much safer. That is partly due to the Channel Tunnel. Residents only ten years ago watched in fascination as barges dredged up thousands of tons from the dreaded Goodwin sandbanks which was then mixed with sea water and pumped via a canvas pipeline up Hospital Hill to Cheriton to provide the foundations for the tunnel terminus sited on Radnor land. Having dumped its sand, another canvas pipe returned the sea water to the beach opposite the Sandgate Hotel.

1975 *The popular Riviera Hotel, flats since 1971, closes for expected redevelopment. The new Sir John Moore housing complex is painted black to resemble fishermen's cottages. For an experimental period of one year, Lower Sandgate Road is to be a no through road. The listed Fleur de Lis pub closes in September. The Star and Garter is to be vacated in July when the police training centre closes. A then New York resident, Linda René-Martin, gifts a bench to the village. Sited on the Wilberforce Road green it is inscribed, "For Happy Times in Sandgate."*

1976 *In September the Sandgate Society obtains from Kent County Council a 6 month lease on the old Fire Station at £3 per week and this commences from January 1st 1977. Then by July this finally becomes long term. A December earth tremor and landslip in Vicarage Road affects two houses, Channeldale and Crow's Nest, after their retaining wall crumbled onto the Riviera access Road. A new toilet block opens to replace the old Granville Parade facility.*

Royal Kent Hotel in its heyday

Reg Turnill: The benchmark for ace space reporting

BBC
AIR
CORRESPONDENT

Radnor Cliff: Showing bottom left, the splendid solitude for the various owners of Cliff House and Palm Beach

Loxford Lodge: Replaced by four town houses.

Refurbished: Kent House: Enbrook - then swiftly demolished.

Optimism: Then the housing market plummeted.

1977 Planning permission is granted for Encombe House to be converted for hotel use. A 35p concessionary bus fare is offered to pensioners. Ridge House on the Undercliff is sold for £8000. The 1 cwt 8 qtrs Fire Station bell, stored at Folkestone museum for safety reasons, is saved by the Society after KCC wished to sell it for £1. It was cast in 1884, has a diameter of 18" and sounds a G musical note. Sydney De Haan buys the Enbrook Estate including the Star and Garter building for £200,000. In September the council attempts to serve notice for immediate repairs to Channeldale and Crow's Nest houses, both now considered dangerous.

1978 A planning application for a holiday site housing 200 caravans on the MOD land at Hospital Hill is refused. The empty 1866 School opens as the Gee Bee Antiques Centre. The Sandgate Hotel reverts back to its original name the Wellington Hotel. In October Encombe House is destroyed in a mystery fire. Bruce Cheeseman, the owner for nine years, confidently claimed, "We should still be able to build on the land. It would be an excellent site for high class housing."

Sandgate Castle

The entrance to the charming little museum.

Since 2000 the converted Castle has been a private residence.

A warm atmosphere for patrons, but a relentless chill for the then owners

1979 *There are calls for fencing around the Sandgate Martello Tower 7 after a junior soldier slipped 30ft down into the moat. Castle Road, closed since April 1977 because of land slippage and the application of 430 tons of shingle to support the 40 foot retaining wall, leads to a £40 rates reduction for residents of Beach Marine. Work should be completed by the summer.*

1980 *The 2 bedroomed Toll House on Lower Sandgate Road is to be sold. In June the Amoco service station starts to sell bicycles.*

Three dining rooms and a function suite made the Castle a unique destination

Castle interior showing the original Tudor Well and steps in the North-East Bastion

1981 The Housing Association behind the Sir John Moore flats owes money to the government and the block is sold on the open market to reduce the £1m debt. The Sandgate Society co-ordinates a fund raising appeal for £1000 to repair the Chichester Hall clock after its gears seized up three years before.

1982 The Sandgate Society may have to vacate the old Fire Station HQ by September. However Socialview Ltd, later the Sandgate Heritage Trust Ltd, led by Geoffrey Edmunds, manages to buy the building for £18,100 . A further £24,000 will be needed for repairs and improvements. Spade House is for sale at £200,000 and is subsequently converted to a care home for 27 patients.

Easy Times on the High Street

Butcher Ken Morris at Number 94.

Next door at 92 was Unwin's Wine Store.

Fresh bread and cakes at 30a.

Showler's Greengrocers at No.74.

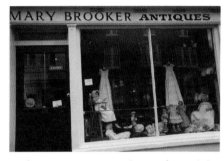
Antiques at No. 39: Another saviour of the High Street.

Fleur de Lis: Once a smuggler's haunt.

The well stocked Pharmacy at Number 37.

A comprehensive choice of High Street shops.

The Cronin's ran the Newsagents at 98.

Keith Holly and daughter Deborah behind the counter at Number 30, Halletts Hardware.

Ron Tabor the popular butcher at Number 38.

Jonathan Greenwall's antiques market ran at 61-63 for 25 years from 1985.

1983 *The freehold of the old School is finally put on the market at £78,000. The annual Ruby Greenwall lecture in memory of the Society's founder is instituted in this the 21st year since formation.*

1984 *The first awards are made in the young people's writing competition named in memory of Lola Lachlan. A former colleague Dr. Alan Fisk, donates £335 worth of Treasury Stock paying interest of nearly 10% to fund the prizes. In December the short road from the High Street down the side of the Royal Norfolk Hotel is named Lachlan Way in memory of the family. The Manor House on Military Road becomes a nursing home. A centenary supper is held in the old Fire Station to celebrate its opening in June 1884. A £1m housing complex for the elderly is to be built opposite the Little Theatre.*

Weather

1965: Strong Winds.

December 1981: Road Closure.

February 1983: High Street flooded.

The Coastguard Cottages under water in 1961.

Solution: Open the archway doors and allow sea water to flow through.

Ship Inn: Beer remains the main attraction.

November 1967: The full fury of the waves block the Esplanade.

Undermined: The Sir John Moore Memorial in 1949.

November 1967: Flooding at Western Esplanade.

Spectacular tides in January 1965.

1985 The Grade II listed old School at the foot of Sandgate Hill is sold in May. Within a year minor external work, the removal of two chimney stacks, is followed by conversion of the building into six separate homes.

1986 Lloyds Bank on the High Street closes on 29th August.

From Conamur to Zarena Court

Built as a private residence in 1896, Conamur (its original name) was leased a year later for use as a school mostly for girls but occasionally for young boys as well. In its first year under Miss F.S. Jarvis, it had very few pupils but gradually increased its roll as news spread of the high quality education.

As it expanded the school also absorbed property either side, with the school opening with The Nook and later adding Audley Cottage. During the First World War the school moved to safer quarters near Bath. After the war and back in Sandgate, the sisters Dora and Lucy Pennycuick ran the school until its closure.

From the school magazine it is clear that school life was highly enjoyable. Trips around Kent were often scheduled and the pupils were regular participants in community events around Sandgate.

Sporting activity ranged from summer swimming to inter-college competitions played locally on their own field at the western end of the Leas until this

A classroom at the well respected Conamur School.

was sold for housing in 1931. Lifelong friendships were made during term time and reunions for past pupils were highly anticipated.

By the 1930s there was a mood change in the country. Gaiety in the twenties was replaced by

Conamur fronting the beach - seen here as The Riviera Hotel.

1987 *Saga proposes converting Enbrook House into a leisure centre, together with the construction of 148 houses on the estate. Plans for a Hythe Marina fuel huge opposition, and lead to a decade long battle. Fresh proposals in 2012 for 150 houses on the historic Princes Parade site suggest the start of another major battle.*

1988 *From October group tours of the Castle can be arranged. In June construction firm Wimpey acquires the Enbrook estate.*

relentless pessimism as the financial world mirrored America's experience. Anxiety was also raised by European politics and the threat of war. For Conamur it meant fewer pupils and in 1936 the Principals sent out this note to pupils and parents.

The School entrance on the Riviera.

A LETTER FROM THE MISSES PENNYCUICK.

Conamur,

May 28th, 1936.   Sandgate.

After long and careful consideration we have decided that the time has come to close Conamur as a school. Naturally this decision causes us deep sorrow but it has been forced upon us by the circumstances of the last few years.

The loss of the ground on the Leas, the drift at an earlier age to the Public Schools, and the demand for a specialised type of building, have made us feel that it is impossible to maintain Conamur as a worthy standard.

We think it better to close it now than to let it sink into a lower place. We know that the spirit of Conamur will not be lost : and, like Miss Jarvis, the school's honoured founder, we shall always have the interest of the Old Girls at heart.

We hope that they will all realise what a true joy it will be to us if they will keep in touch with us and come and see us when they can. We hope to live at Silourie and shall look forward to welcoming many old girls and members of the Staff in the future.

D. and L. PENNYCUICK.

To the sadness of everyone the school closed at the end of the summer term. The Misses Pennycuick lived here for another year until the lease was sold in 1938 and the former school became the Riviera Hotel.

The Conamur School lasted 39 years – the Riviera Hotel a similar time before closing, along with many other hotels in the district. By this time air travel offered holiday visitors more predictable summer weather. At the same time local land values had risen and redevelopment loomed. The Riviera Hotel building closed, eventually to be replaced in 1986 by the attractive Zarena Court complex. Different eras, different preferences.

Conamur: Seabathing but only at 60°F

1989 *Wimpey plan construction of 104 houses, flats and roads at Enbrook but work is postponed because of market conditions. In February the Eurotunnel exhibition centre opens at Cheriton. The local doctor's surgery and the 150 year old Pharmacy close. In July Radnor Cliff residents complain of nude bathing on the beach.*

1990 *The village faces the onslaught of a February storm. Builders Wimpey pull out of the Enbrook development. The Amoco Petrol site is leased to Jet for 2 years but an application was previously lodged to demolish this and the adjacent Corunna House. Work starts in June on the land stabilisation plan - with the delivery from Luxembourg of 14 dowel piles.*

1925 School Photograph

A Lesson in Good Design.

One of Sandgate Society's major successes was the campaign to save the Church of England Primary School at the foot of Sandgate Hill. In 1972 when the school closed, the land ownership reverted to the Radnor Estate. This land had been deeded following a government campaign to introduce formal education for all classes. The landed gentry were encouraged to assist in this worthy aim, and they enthusiastically agreed to provide practical space for new schools.

Education for those not part of the elite was fragmented and was mainly offered by enlightened members of the clergy. Here in Sandgate a regular visitor, William Wilberforce, was at the forefront of help for the illiterate. Alongside his opposition to the slave trade, he also used his Evangelical calling to promote basic education for the poor. His efforts led to an informal Adult school set up in a surplus Ordnance storeroom around 1814. Chapel Street School was also established at this time with Henry Butcher as Headmaster. Later, after 1820, the school moved to rented rooms near Martello Cottages.

Additional facilities grew from here and by 1844, following the School Sites Act (1841), a larger hall, adjacent to the Castle became Sandgate's first National School, on land deeded by Lord Radnor and built to the designs of Edward Gotto.

As the population grew in the village, a new school was erected by 1866 again on Radnor land and with the sole funding from James Morris of Encombe. It was designed by Philip Charles Hardwick, son and grandson of an architectural dynasty, including Thomas and Philip, and whose notable work also included the great hall at Euston Station, The Great Western Hotel, Paddington Station and the gothic revival Beauchamp Almshouses and Chapel at Newlands, Worcestershire.

The new Sandgate School was formally opened in June 1866 and classes commenced from 2nd September. Its weekly charge of 1d was a tenth of the price of education in Folkestone – and quickly attracted many from western parts of the town.

The education reformers were delighted with progress here and across the country. In an early report, Sandgate's School was described by an Inspector as "very commodious and, in respect of beauty, without rival in the district." The Reformers and Inspectors would, however, be quite dismayed to learn that today 20% of young people end their school life lacking basic skills in literacy and numeracy.

1991 *The results of a traffic count through Sandgate do not justify a hoped for pedestrian crossing near the Ship Inn. A Green walk is proposed from the old Cheriton Railway Station to Sandgate Castle but is opposed by individual householders. Rocks from Norway are delivered for the sea groynes.*

1992 *The Chichester Hall Trust takes over the management of the hall from Shepway District Council in April. Geoffrey Edmunds leads a campaign to reopen the paths across the barracks, closed two years ago amid IRA terrorism threats.*

May 1988: Three cottages already sold.

School Class of 1957.

Life at the old School must have been a joy for children with a thirst for learning. Many youngsters had perfect attendance records – in 1900 Ellen Finnis was awarded a medal for perfect attendance over nine years, while in 1902 T. Moore was awarded a gold medal for his 12 years of perfect time keeping. Stepping forward to the early 1970s we find that the Dioceses of Canterbury found maintaining the facility too costly and took a decision to sell the Primary School. At this point, under the terms of the deed, the land would legally revert to Radnor ownership. The Estate cast around for an alternative owner and use but after considerable time and effort, concluded that the only solution was to sell the freehold. An auction was set for September 1976, but three years earlier, a Grade II listing had been obtained, limiting the scope of development.

From the School's closure, the Sandgate Society had mounted a vigorous campaign to save the building for community use and, after many years of thwarted redevelopment applications, the Radnor Estate attempted to reach a sensible compromise with the village.

Fortuitously in 1974 a House of Lords bill promoted community use of such buildings, but it wasn't until 1986, after intervention by the Secretary of State, that permission was granted for a development of six cottages – with no need for part demolition of the School as previously proposed by the Estate.

An exceptionally sympathetic design was produced for the new owner, David O'Clee, by local architect Roger Joyce. Adding to the heritage statement, each of the dwellings was named after a Headmaster or Mistress who had so successfully steered the School to outstanding achievement.

The cottages, Neale, Woods, White, Ulyett, Dexter and Glandfield have proved to be attractive and popular dwellings – with a corresponding increase in asking price from £90,000 in 1987 to today's £250,000. The foresight of the original village campaigners to save the old School for the village has also retained a legacy of distinction at Sandgate's eastern entrance.

1993 On Saturday 20th February the new village sign, mainly funded by a legacy from the late Miss Hornsby, and designed and erected by the Society, is unveiled by the Town Mayor. A campaign starts for a pedestrian crossing outside the Little Theatre. Construction begins of a bar on the first floor of the Restaurant Boleyn after a restriction on the supply of intoxicating liquors, inserted to protect the trading position of the Providence Inn, was lifted in November 1989. Encombe stabilisation work continues with the eventual sinking of 164 dowel piles at the toe of the landslip. In November Saga buys back its Enbrook landholding.

1994 The height of the new shingle beach shows a downside by not being naturally cleansed by the sea - plus keeping the gangway path clear costs £3,000 a year.

Saga of the Recycled Castle

Henry VIII, oddly one of Phil Spector's all time heroes, was 500 years ahead of the green movement in Kent. Having dissolved the monasteries, he set about building Sandgate Castle with stone recycled from mostly St. Radigunds Priory near Dover, the Christ Church Canterbury and Monk's Horton. The 147 thousand bricks were carted up and down the hills to this solitary location with only William Jenkin's house as company. This building, partly retained within the Fleur de Lis, was hired for use as the King's pay house for 900 workers on the two year project with completion on 2nd October 1540. In the following March the King dropped in to inspect his creation, and again in May 1542 met and dined with Folkestone dignitaries.

Lord of the Manor, Lord Clinton, was appointed Captain of the Castle in 1553. Sir Henry Clinton, a 19th century relative of his, was a brother of Augusta , wife of Henry Dawkins, the first owner of the Encombe Estate in Sandgate.

Queen Elizabeth dined and rested at the Castle in 1573 on her journey from Westenhanger to Dover. Then in September 1617 a major part of the front sea wall was damaged in a storm. By 1694, Lord of the Manor, Sir Basil Dixwell, was Captain of the Castle. Just three years later he sold his massive landholding in the district to the future Radnor dynasty.

The 19th century saw the deterioration and demolition of the central "Queen's Chamber" and its conversion to a giant Martello Tower, completed on 20th August 1805. The War Office relinquished control of the Castle in May 1881 and sold it for £20,000 to the S.E. Railway Company who held an unfulfilled plan to extend their line from Sandgate to Folkestone. By 1893 the Castle was opened as a tourist attraction by the Sandgate Improvement Association who took a peppercorn lease from the railway company. A small but fascinating museum was kept in the Porter's Lodge until 1928 when the Castle was again sold, together with Castle Close, to M.A. Batchelor of Bleak House, Broadstairs. By 1936 it was included in the sale of Castle Close (c.1910) owned by W.A.Allen.

SANDGATE CASTLE FOR SALE

SANDGATE Castle is included with Castle Close, which will be offered for sale by Temple, Barton Ltd., at the Queen's Hotel on Wednesday, November 10th.

Mr. W. A. Workman, owner of Castle Close and the Castle, has given instructions for the properties to be sold.

The Castle was eventually scheduled as an ancient monument in 1939. Ironically in 1949, the year it gained Grade 1 listing, a fierce storm reduced the remaining south wall to rubble. The then owner W.A.Workman sold his house and the Castle at auction in November 1954 to Shorncliffe Lodge resident, Frederick Black. His family later came to bitterly regret the purchase. "The Castle went with this house. We had to buy the wretched place. We had to take the lot at the time. We wish we could find someone to perhaps open it up as a restaurant." The properties cost Mr. Black £5,000 and were purchased for his daughter Barbara, a medical student.

SANDGATE CASTLE APPLICATION

Block of flats on site proposed

APPLICATION to demolish Sandgate Castle and build a block of flats on the site has been refused. The castle is scheduled as an ancient monument.

The application for "outline" planning permission for Dr. B. L. McGregor envisaged two eight-storey blocks of 32 flats and two blocks of eight garages.

The planning authority, refusing the application, say there would be excessive population density, over-development of the land and congestion of buildings, insufficient garaging and parking accommodation for cars, lack of space within the curtilage of the site for garden amenities.

SCHEDULED

They also point out that the castle is a scheduled ancient monument and included in the list of buildings of special architectural or historical interest.

An "outline" application for the demolition of nearby "Castle Close" and the erection of an eight-storey block of 32 flats with eight garages for Dr. McGregor has also been refused.

Reasons are that the population density would be excessive, there would be overdevelopment of the land and congestion of buildings, insufficient garaging and car parking, lack of space for garden amenities.

Folkestone Herald : 3/1/1962.

1995 Ruby Greenwall, founder of the Sandgate Society, dies. Power boats are banned within 200m from the low water mark. Suncliffe House, a new name for Endcliffe House, was sold for £212,500 in January.

1996 Enbrook is demolished in January after a vigorous battle by the Society to save the listed building. Residents celebrate the centenary of the Coastguard Cottages. The Admiralty took a 65 year lease from the Radnor Estate in February 1896. The freehold was sold at auction to a speculator in 1952, who, when facing financial debts six years later, sold this on to individual cottage owners at an inflated price. The village was drenched in a once in 500 year event, with 4 inches of rain falling on Monday 12th August. Beach replenishment is completed in August at a cost of £18m. Tributes are paid to former Chairman of the Society, Dennis Vorley, who dies in December.

major tourist attraction. Ominously in 1974 Peter became responsible for a bank loan, taken out by Barbara's father, which held a full legal obligation to restore the listed Castle.

Over the next 14 years of renovation their debts ballooned to £650,000 - in addition to their £200,000 personal investment. Then in 1976 the McGregors appear to have taken a lease on the old Saga Club, formerly the Fleur De Lis, for use as the Boleyn Restaurant .

By 1989 they purchased the freehold taking an additional loan in 1991 from Lloyds Bank.

Although the Castle reopened to the public in 1983 and the restaurant and Dungeon coffee shop were proving popular, the debts became overwhelming as a Lloyds Bank spokesperson explained. "The family ran various businesses which were all trading at a loss. It got to the point that the debt was such that we went to court in 1995 for permission to repossess the Castle and the Restaurant Boleyn, and this was granted."

Dogged by debt and facing financial collapse, Dr. Peter McGregor took an overdose of barbiturates and died three months later of a lung infection. Lloyds Bank described the situation as "A very sad case. Because of what she has been through we said that Dr. Barbara McGregor could stay in her home at the Restaurant Boleyn for as long as she pleases."

Dramatically in January 1962 the owners applied to demolish the Castle and replace it with two eight-storey blocks of 32 flats and two blocks of eight garages. They also applied for a similar scheme to follow the demolition of Castle Close house. Both schemes were refused.

By the 1970s Dr. Peter McGregor, following a serious accident, took early retirement and together with his wife Barbara (daughter of Frederick Black) were looking for a new consuming interest. The couple's thoughts turned to possibly reopening the Castle as a

1997 *In January Lloyds Bank forecloses on Sandgate Castle. The old telephone exchange in the North Lane is converted into 3 flats.*

1998 *Work on the new Saga building at Enbrook is nearing completion and staff will move in by November. Reg Chapman's Hardware Store closes in September. Reg Turnill and Geoffrey Edmunds continue to campaign for the MOD to reopen the northerly footpath over Shorncliffe Camp closed because of the IRA menace. St.Mark's Church Shorncliffe closes after the final service on 11th November. Sandgate Castle, on the market for a year, finally sells for £300,000. The Library reopens in August, a year after being flooded.*

Riches along the Radnor Road

"Folkestone produced a decent income, including a toll on all the crabs landed at the harbour." - **Jacob, 4th Earl 1815 - 1889.**

The des Bouverie family were originally silk traders in the Spanish Netherlands. Here the Catholic Huguenots faced persecution and the Bouveries fled first to Frankfurt, then France and eventually to Sandwich in Kent.

By the 17th century they were well established in this country. The son of Sir Edward des Bouverie, Jacob, acquired the Honour and Lordship of Folkestone and Terlingham from Sir Basil Dixwell who had inherited the land in 1622 from an uncle. Dixwell held more interest in his landholding around Canterbury where he built Broome House. He did keep a link with the south coast when elected as MP for Hythe in 1626 and High Sheriff of Kent the following year. His son, also Sir Basil, was later Captain of Sandgate Castle.

This sale of 2,577 acres to the Bouverie family for £19,500 included the whole of Sandgate as far as the western end of Coastguard Cottages. Even the early shipbuilders here had to lease space on the seashore.

Sir William des Bouverie (1656-1717) was by 1707 a Governor of the Bank of England and knighted some five years later. He formalised the leasehold system in Folkestone which led to very

Why Earl Radnor keeps drawbridge up on public

LORD Radnor explained this week why he does not open his country castle to the public. And one of the deciding factors was that people would make the place smell.

His triangular-shaped castle in Wiltshire did not have a wing where he could shut himself off, he told a Folkestone and district Junior Chamber of Commerce luncheon.

"The people who come round may be very nice, but you don't want to see or hear them all the time," said Lord Radnor.

"I am told that you can even smell them. Eventually your house takes on an odour, rather like a station."

However, his castle was opened to the public for charity purposes.

But he did not want to get too deeply involved. "I feel that, in this particular castle, the people would destroy its soul," he added.

"If you open the lodge gates you can't just say, 'Oh! well, I'm only going to have 100 through today.'

"You have just got to take what comes."

controlled development of the town, including the creation of generous green spaces still enjoyed by residents. In the year that Sir William died his son Edward (1688-1736) purchased Longford Castle. Sir Jacob des Bouverie (1694-1761) was created Ist Viscount Folkestone and his son Jacob was honoured to become Ist Earl of Radnor later marrying Harriet Pleydell. When she died young, her land holdings inheritance went to son Jacob (1750-1828), who in 1776 inherited the title 2nd Earl of Radnor.

William, the 3rd Earl (1779-1869) was regarded as generous to the Folkestone township, providing land for schools and churches - although it is said he was wise (or wily) enough to insert reverter clauses in many of the deeds of gift. He confirmed later, "Folkestone was important. The revenues that came from there were substantial and from many quarters." By 1860 the family was also the largest shareholder in the Folkestone Water Works Company, of which the Estate architect Sydney Smirke was Chairman.

The architecture of the new development was initially laid out by Decimus Burton, but the bulk of the building design was undertaken by Burton's former class friend, Sydney Smirke. His work in Folkestone barely merits a mention in the Victorian Society's book, 'Seven Victorian Architects' with only Christ Church being noted. Smirke is then rather unkindly dismissed as "a first class, second rate architect."

1999 *Refurbishment plans are announced to convert the Castle into a luxury four bedroomed residence with the roof patterned on Hospital Hill's Martello 8, and a three car garage based on the design of the Sea Cadets HQ. Geoffrey Boot, the new owner, spends a considerable sum on taking the Castle off the English Heritage "at risk" register. Former President and Chairman of the Society, Geoffrey Edmunds, dies in June. The village Christmas Lights are switched on by East Enders actress Patsy Palmer.*

2000 *Work is completed on the conversion of the Castle. Westbury Homes start building work at the former MOD site on Hospital Hill. Gurkhas start to arrive at Shorncliffe Camp. Former head of Radio One and BBC2 TV, Sandgate born Robin Scott dies in February aged 79 . Craig Fairbrass from East Enders switches on the village Christmas lights.*

Jacob, known as the Viscount Folkestone from 1889, had addresses at Longford Castle, in London at 52 Grosvenor Street and at 31 Augusta Gardens, Folkestone (Augusta was his grandmother's name). After marriage in 1891, and the start of a growing family, the Manor House in Earl's Avenue was built and occupied from around 1898. He inherited the 6th Earldom of Radnor in 1900 and became Folkestone's Town Mayor the following year. Then in 1907, with 8 children, the family moved to Cliff House. Two further offspring were born at Cliff House, where a new east wing provided the Lord and Lady with separate bedrooms.

Land leases around the area could extend to 999 years, such as the one the town still holds on the cliffs between Folkestone and Sandgate. A term of 99 years on a house would be quite normal – with many containing a "tenancy for life" clause held by the landowner. One purchaser of a freehold in Radnor Park Avenue in 1912 had to indemnify the Earl against any death duty claims arising on his late father's estate. The freehold of land under a leasehold property could be sold at auction in London with no reference to the local occupiers, such was the case with the Coastguard Cottages in Sandgate.

Even a freehold property on Radnor land still needs written consent from the Estate office

The 6th Earl of Radnor: Mayor of Folkestone 1901 - 1902.

before any change or usage is permitted. By the 1990s annual revenue from the area amounted to £1 million.

The Radnor family also has considerable land interests in London around Whitefriars and Fleet Street, hence Pleydell Street and Bouverie Street. A development in the latter is on a 150 year lease and the full freehold interest will revert to the family in 2151. As Jacob the 8th Earl remarked, "The game then continues."

2001 *Ridge House on the Undercliff (boarded up for 15 years) is considered an eyesore and dangerous and faces council pressure for demolition - it was gone by January 2002. Coolinge House is left in a will to a donkey sanctuary. East Enders actor Adam Woodyatt is the final star to switch on the village Christmas lights because of high costs. The Encombe bathing house was auctioned in February for £65,000. Former resident Professor Dame Sheila Sherlock F.R.S., the country's leading liver specialist, dies in December aged 83.*

2002 *Initial moves are made for twinning with Sangatte. Geoffrey Boot the new owner of the Castle invites the Sandgate Society to enjoy its barbecue in the grounds. Saga is asked to use Sandgate in their address instead of Folkestone. A controversial house on Hospital Hill gains retrospective planning permission for exceeding the original dimensions. Joan Thompson and Brenda Georgiou retire after years of loyal service to the Society. Riviera Road is sold at auction in September with a guide price of £12,000. The land was acquired in 1888 and the Radnor Estate registered the Freehold in 2000. The new owner will have the right to grant access to any new development along and beyond the road. The Village celebrates the Golden Jubilee with a week of events from 31st May.*

Earth Slips

September 1991: Landslip below Vicarage Road

There has been a history of land slippage around Sandgate for hundreds of years. This is caused by the geological combination of a hard lower shelf, with a clay upper section slowly sliding seaward by gravity. The major disaster in 1893 showed the power of nature when many houses simply crumbled during the event. Steel piling has since been used in more contemporary structures, but some older houses contain an unwelcome surprise for new owners. The existence of numerous springs simply adds to the potential instability.

In 1968 after much local pressure, Folkestone Town Council agreed to fund two boreholes to investigate the recent slips around the Encombe area but who should pay for this would become a long running saga. Councillor Jack Sainsbury explained, "Years ago I made requests for council houses to be built at Wilberforce Road and in Encombe Valley, and the reports I received at the time suggested these sites were not appropriate for new building. The recent slips occurred on

1893 : The end of Spring House

private property." He then added ominously, "The responsibility must lie with the owners, developers and builders of property on this land, and with the people who made searches on behalf of the property holders."

Rodney Court wall

During the initial Council investigation reference was made to the 1958 Halcrow report (for a previous owner, for another purpose) which stated that if property was not built on or near the 1893 slip then the houses would not behave any differently to houses east and west which survived that landslip.

When developers had bought the Encombe Estate in 1962 they quickly ruined the water features that had previously supplied the Sandgate Laundry. Many trees and shrubs were also cut down destabilising the soil covering even more.

An earth tremor in 1976 led to land slippage above the Riviera, and as late as 2012 excavations for a new development adjacent to this site on Vicarage Road created a massive mud slide into Radnor Cliff Crescent.

2003 *The village Post Office closes in August. De-trunking of the busy coastal road (A259) is finally achieved in October. The first 3 and 4 bedroomed houses are released in September on the Ocean Ridge/Hospital Hill development.*

2004 *Gilcrest Homes Ltd pays £800,000 for the old Sea Cadets HQ after an energetic campaign to save this former 1845 National School. Permission is sought to build 5 One Bedroomed Town Houses on the virtually empty Kirby Arcade shopping site. Coastal protection requires 200,000 tons of rocks to be laid along the coast from Folkestone to Hythe. In July a service is held at St. Paul's Church to mark the official twinning with the French coastal town Sangatte. Nicola, daughter of Roger Joyce, swims the channel completing 24 miles in 14 hours 15 minutes.*

Sandgate's Little Theatre

The Folkestone Dramatic & Music Club was formed in 1902 and used the Woodward Institute for its productions. By 1913 an Operatic Society had been created, and in 1946 the Society was restarted after the war with Hythe now added to the name. Performances were also presented at the Leas Pavilion Theatre, the Pleasure Gardens Theatre, the Town Hall, the Odeon Cinema and in Sandgate's Chichester Hall. The society's first permanent base was a 57 seater in the Queen's Hotel Annexe on Church Street – this became Ham Yard from 1952.

The cast of Hobson's Choice takes the final curtain call.

2006: The last audience.

When Sandgate's 1883 Congregational Church closed in 1964 it created a chance for FHODS to expand and a subsequent lease was agreed. After extensive refurbishment, the first production took the stage on 24th January 1966. Margaret Dawe's production of Molières "The Imaginary Invalid" played to packed houses during its run and the 100 seat theatre continued to offer a mix of stimulating entertainment for the next four decades.

By 1993 bigger productions required a more extensive scenery store, workshop and rehearsal space and the group took over a warehouse in Gough Road, recently vacated by Halletts hardware store. Meanwhile up at Shorncliffe, the MOD was preparing to sell the former St. Mark's Church, built between 1939 and 1941 by Otto Marx Ltd, a German firm, based in Folkestone. Oddly within days of opening for services, Lord Haw Haw announced that the Church would soon be bombed. Bullet holes at the eastern end still confirm an attack.

For the Society such a spacious open canvas was a great temptation. With this in mind their Gough Road premises in Sandgate were sold in 2001, and after winning the sealed bid, FHODS became the proud owner of the future Tower Theatre. Much effort and funding was required to fit out this new theatre and entertainment complex and it was to be another five years before the theatre could open. In the meantime the Little Theatre continued to thrive – with the final performance of Hobson's Choice on Saturday 27th May 2006 ending a forty year presence on Sandgate High Street. The building was put up for auction during the final week and sold for £220,000.

Less than two months later the new Tower Theatre opened. All 100 seats, loaned from the Folkestone School for Girls, and placed on the church flagstone floor, were sold out for a celebration of musicals in "Showtime '06" from Monday 8th July 2006. Since then a varied programme has catered for all artistic tastes – with the New Year Pantomime being a traditional highlight. The raked seating, on a new floor, was gradually installed and now offers a theatre capacity of 290.

2005 *Another campaign starts to open up the seawall walkway (the maintenance gangway) from Sandgate to Folkestone for public use. Although Shepway District Council has a 999 lease on the land, it remains in Radnor Estate control - a position that exists to this day - with use of the walkway at public risk. Gordon Ramsay films an episode of Kitchen Nightmares at the Sandgate Hotel in June. Sadly the hotel closed at the end of the year with debts of £250,000 - two months before the show was broadcast.*

2006 *Planning permission is granted for flats to replace Coolinge House, considered a rare example of an early Georgian farmhouse. The first recipient of the Reg Turnill Plate award for service to the Society was Linda René-Martin. During her acceptance speech she refers to herself as a PIN - Perpetual Infernal Nuisance.*

A History of Enbrook House
Compiled by Chris Phillips

At a time when the village of Sandgate was becoming a popular intimate resort, John, 4th Earl of Darnley (1767-1831) of Cobham Hall bought the grounds at Enbrook and built a marine villa. Also in 1822 he added a Chapel of Ease. On his death in 1831 his second son, Hon. John Duncan Bligh, inherited the property. The original house had been embellished over the years but was pulled down in 1852 and the familiar new mansion was constructed in the centre of the estate – to the designs of Samuel S. Teulon. After living in the house for twenty years, John Bligh died and the estate was inherited by his only daughter, Countess of Chichester, the wife of Walter, Lord Pelham 4th Earl of Chichester. The Countess died in 1911 and Sandgate's Chichester Hall was built in her memory.

The estate ownership transferred to Major L.E. Bligh who, within a year, put the property up for auction. However it failed to sell and records do not detail its use during the First World War, but in 1919 it was sold to the Red Cross who reopened it within a year as their Star and Garter Home for injured service personnel. Then when refurbishment of their Richmond house was completed by 1924, Enbrook House was rebuilt to the designs of Sir Edwin Cooper, as a holiday home for the disabled of World War 1.

Enbrook House reopened in 1928 and showed a Cape Dutch style with rectangular rooms and neat stuccoed walls. The port corchère and nearby chimney from the Teulon designed building remained and now highlighted two very different architectural styles.

Enbrook from 1928 incorporating the original portico to east. To the rear is Kent House.

During the Second World War the building was evacuated and leased to the Home Office for use as both training and stores for the National Fire Service. From 1946 it became one of eight provincial police training centres. As No.6 District, it encompassed Kent, Sussex, Surrey, Hampshire, Berkshire and the Isle of Wight. In those days and until the merger in 1967, no fewer than thirteen

The 1852 private house and the public Church (built 1849) complemented each other on the attractive Enbrook Estate.

2007 *Permission is refused to convert the old Little Theatre into 5 town houses. The building then goes back on the market at twice the previous auction price and a further application permits dwellings without parking spaces. Dave (later Davina) the Dolphin becomes a popular tourist attraction on the coast between Sandgate and Seabrook.*

2008 *The Gurkha Regiment is proud to accept the Freedom of Sandgate. All the shops in the Kirby Arcade face imminent demolition for a, so far unfulfilled, plan to build town houses without parking.*

forces were catered for at Enbrook as most counties contained small forces with County Borough status. As well as basic police training, Enbrook also offered student instructor courses and, due to its location, was also used by colonial and foreign police forces.

In 1977 the estate was purchased by Saga who for a decade used it as offices. Staff increases then made it too small and it was sold to the builders, Wimpey. Site plans were drawn up to develop the area with an Hotel, a sports centre, a restaurant and a nursing home. A later plan included over three hundred houses

The Star & Garter Home was here from 1920 before the major rebuilding project four years later.

and these would entail the demolition of the Commandant's house on Sandgate Hill to ease access to the grounds.

At this time though, the housing market was stagnant and Wimpey, after refurbishing and advertising the Kent House development, sold the estate back to Saga. The Enbrook House Grade 2

listing, obtained in March 1975, was removed and all buildings on the estate were demolished by 1993.

Designed by Sir Michael Hopkins, Saga's iconic new edifice was then ready for business from November 1998. The Pavilion was offered for community use and there remains highly valued public access to the well maintained verdant grounds.

Sea Point: Originally built in 1912 as a bungalow, it was later a Refreshment Centre and bathing establishment from 1931 to 1949 before destruction in a massive storm.

2009 *Reg Turnill forms the H.G. Wells Literary Award Scheme. The Sea Festival is to become a Sea and Food weekend with fireworks an added attraction.*

2010 *Ambitious plans for art and drama are proposed for the area around the Sir John Moore memorial. The Sea Point Cafe stood to the west of this site but was demolished in 1949. The present amphitheatre section was then constructed for deck chairs and sheltered sun bathing as part of the sea wall defences completed by 1953. Construction of the H.G.Wells memorial seat for the Green is completed. (Project: Linda René-Martin)*

July 1977

Let's Go Shopping

This month in... SANDGATE

Where there's time for friendly service

JUBILEE flags flutter in friendly Sandgate High Street.

AT FIRST glance, Sandgate's High Street seems to hold little for the housewife whose shopping list is not headed by antiques of every shape, size and age.

But there is much in this pretty seaside shopping centre to warrant a closer look.

It is a local bone of contention that the village does not have a bakery.

Nevertheless, what is missing in the way of pastries is more than made up for by the friendliness and informality of the High Street.

Unlike the crowded centre in nearby Folkestone, people have time to wander around to look for what they want without being jostled.

There are high quality butcher's and fishmonger's shops.

Randlesome's delicatessen at the Seabrook end of the village can offer the best, and the slightly unusual, in provisions.

And there are two grocery shops for the fruit and veg, both of which sell bread (and coal for that matter!)

Collins hardware shop stocks everything from buckets to lettuce seeds, and retains the old-fashioned air of service with a smile that seems sadly missing from modern shops.

Lukey's, the wine merchants, stock the expected beers and spirits, and they have an excellent range of wines to suit all pockets.

A visit to Fred Moore's shoe shop has added benefits aside from getting those leaking shoes mended.

For he sells a nice line in potted plants, including cacti.

And more of the unexpected. A trip to Sandgate could well get you interested in Windsurfing.

The Windsurfers' club has opened a shop in the High Street where surfboards and literature are available.

Sandgate also boasts a pottery and a yoga centre tucked away **behind** Sandgate Motors' showrooms.

Locals bemoan the fact that, a few years ago, the village had three more pubs than it does now.

But thirsty shoppers in need of refreshment can choose between The Norfolk Hotel, The Ship and The Providence — as well as The Clarendon in Brewer's Hill.

And for those in need of something more solid, the newly-opened Caverna 91 Restaurant in the High Street offers superb Italian food and wine at remarkably low prices.

Proprietor Georgio Rossi's home made cakes and confectionery are out of this world!

And if antiques are at the top of your shopping list, then what better place to go than Sandgate?